THIS IS HOW HE LEFT ME

Jennifer Hook

Workwomans Press
Seattle

This Is How He Left Me © Jennifer Hook 2014
All Rights Reserved

Cover Design by Jennifer Hook

ISBN 978-0-9820073-8-9
First Printing October 2014

Workwomans Press
Seattle
www.workwomanspress.com

THIS IS HOW HE LEFT ME

GARY AYRES
April 20, 1957 - October 21, 2010

for Gary

Contents

GOOD MORNING 1
STATE 2
HEAVENLY BLUE 3
5/21/2011 4
MEMORIAL DAY 5
RELATIVE HUMIDITY 6
PLAN 7
EARTH'S BODY 8
300 DAYS 9
SLEEPER 10
UNTITLED 11
GLACIAL ERRATICS SETTLED FOR A TIME 12-13
THIS IS HOW HE LEFT ME 14
GOOD MORNING, DEATH 15
ANNIVERSARY 16
ELEGY 17
KINDS OF NOTHING 18
SEPTEMBER 19
A PLACE IN THE UNIVERSE 20
Notes
The Author

GOOD MORNING

The nurse called *come quickly*. I changed clothes
and collected my knitting, not knowing
your beating heart slowed.

I barely arrived
to lay myself down by his side
to lay me down one last time.

You were always so strong
thumping heart beneath breast bone
your endless song my metronome.

I thought of the motherless chimp
wrapped in a single electric blanket and clinging
to a clock, not like you, my devil wind.

I damn you to hell and all your angles
from your Michelangelo
feet to your grizzled archipelago
of burning love. Fuck you.

STATE

I don't want you to think I'm crazy,
but I have to be honest.
If I had no obligations
I would run away from home
a one-way ticket
I don't know where
The West Coast?
Somewhere warm.

Don't you have, could you stay with your dad or your brother,
a place on the lake with your family and lie on the beach
all day. You wouldn't have to worry about your daughter

I'm not in this world.
I promise I'll write when I get there.

Not really. I mean I don't really plan to disappear
I'm a grown up with a job.
I would write, though. I promise.

HEAVENLY BLUE

What day'd I pull down
the end-of-season vines
no more to climb visibly
inching up the twine, not
the lush snap of your stem
but sinewy and brown,
newly but no less gone.

Today I burst between forefinger, thumb
Every burnt out lantern spilling
blackened seeds in my bucket of tears
They fall to rise up again
like Jesus on Easter, push aside
The clods, rise again you morning
glories, launch your assault to the sky

Give me a number; one, for
the hedge, next calculate
the outliers, then Powerball
Lotto, pick four, pick six
There must be some luck
but none for me. Pat seeds
into ground, lets see what comes.

5/21/2011

The stone holds one corner down while the others flutter, crumbs
in pockets a path back home: head, hearth, cherry, soap;
worry, rolling, heart of, sleep like, skipping, and not one unturned.
Who knew these hard knocks were the music of the spheres
you and their glory a paper tongue. She loves them all
near spherical, unlikely tic-tac-toe, the bastard blue sea glass.

I miss your shoulders. Twelve thousand days, twin tides
       weathered together
with millions still scraping the same space, your ghost holds ground
our pits and pocks caught like gears until burnished, second skin.

Stone, my cheek. Stone, my hand. Half stone, half air the prow
breathes and lays into cup of wind: constant, magnificent
elephant's graveyard, calving now.

MEMORIAL DAY

The good news is, the car's not on fire
anymore. Our hips slid, twinning
eastern saunter down any road, my shoulder
velvet box. Snicked mooring hand in
my back pocket. Parachute, your trailing kite ape wings

Morning dove more than ever, I got my hair done.
That's me in the mirror. Got a pedicure
we are equally real, together. Do you feel it
my immortal moving picture? Drinking
margaritas on the beach with Leo Carrillo,
Cheech was Pancho, sidekick to heroic caballero.
L.A., unlike Vermont. People don't stop for poets.

RELATIVE HUMIDITY

 Highest, 97, at 4:00 AM,
we sit out on the grass, lawn chairs
outside the kitchen window.
Whose funeral, whose family picnic spread
lifelike as a breath inhaled
On waking, missed not at all, I thought you
just out of view, around the corner, at
my elbow, under the arbor in the side yard.

So hot cigarettes the only
smell. A nicotine wind
blows off the asphalt and
Tree of Heaven shelters. Twenty
degrees above normal. Another listless drag.
Only drunks fool enough to come outside.

PLAN

I knew a man who stood on a ledge at night. After love-making
consider the breach. Very still,
for a rock climber, his monkey limbs akimbo, heart & brain also.
Gaze, revolving boomerangs for twenty thousand days.

He'd call sometimes: *the key to the safe's
on the ledge by the window.*
One day came home, this lithe stone master who scaled half dome,
flew bouldering through hidden valleys. Lost his grip,
literally, dropped a platter.

The man clambered to the nearest window, stepped
to the ledge, still there. *Too soon, please try
this electron buzz, this unpronounceable cocktail
what's in your pockets*

duct tape, survival blanket, ten inch nails an escape plan should
civil unrest break out.
Should he choose his own time
I vowed to honor his hands and feet.

Riddled, not ready, the freestyle spider
on the first ascent up the face of his final days.
Glorious animal insolence ripping intravenous lines,
wisp of him climbing.
Stand by his witness, gift or betrayal, I didn't steal him away.

EARTH'S BODY

An 8.9 magnitude quake hit Japan and
in my bones you told me again of broken
Alaska in '64, towns tossed aside in heaps
of earth and fishing boats discarded, dead-fish
among dollhouses stripped completely of siding.

I missed you all the way to California, where
the land would fall into the sea. In storms,
we'd go down to the cliffs and hope for drama,
watch the hulks of trees shake the pilings, stroll
the swollen shore at the reach of debris.

Tsunamis travel almost instantaneously, nothing
to stop them in the open sea. The earth is on fire
not really solid, a skin scabbed over. Why the surprise?
We traveled from Orcas to Zuma, every sort of water
sucking down, our rolling footprints sink away.

Sure enough, the tsunami watch was declared from Alaska to Baja,
like-minded worshipers down at Lighthouse Point watched surfers
hoped to feel the shiver of our planet's skin. You'd of been riveted.

The tides are right, the swell is good, the weather is good,
*   the tsunami is there. We're going out.*

300 DAYS

In early Japanese disaster narratives called *mono no aware*,
'the sadness of things' a wind is going to come, and all things
dust, or into the waves. Results we see today are fossils.

What is loss and where does that put you now,
my nothing gone and breaded meat we shared at dusk.
Lamp and a lamp, the civil twilight has its lamps and I your
shadow.

Swallowed all of you I'd even eat the sand of your bones,
urn just there on the shelf. Just a taste of gravel. Why not
suck finger, dip saliva into the jar and raise your silicate.

The taste: first, the hints of butter and finest grit in juices of mussels.
Chips of stone, flavorless on my tongue. And tangy, pinch of salt
        dissolves
with a sip of water. I swallow. Travel along. I wonder: how many
have done this. As always, perhaps I tasted my own skin.

SLEEPER

The trees out
window stained
glass threshing
day, light lying all
the more. Hooded bays
my plaster double-
paned bedroom henge.
The yellowed runnels
curtain queen-
sized observation deck
on planet's wake,
the turning
right on time, its
scheduled run the only
train on time. We
pulled each
other into this.

UNTITLED

A house, a tree and a person on a page
Title it yellow tape, all wrapped
but not the ribbon for a fighting man gone so
much farther

We still have our shoes and sky
through an alley, diminishing facades
our eyes climbing stairs, soul follows
brushing skin where am I traveling

GLACIAL ERRATICS SETTLED FOR A TIME

& another time.
In chill, cry bird, then away

snow's running. Sun commands: go ache in it
hasty, high country blow flute-bottle
gentling belly of a bear-
charging day.

I am your meadow, gone

shamble me another
dry lightning flash a battery &
far but reachable burn
like turf, lay cheek against green beard, high
voices of river pebbles call: me & you,
babe, how about it

one hard pan mile of lupine blazing now.
I never thought weather could be
so horny-toad dog howling dog.

In winter, know torn root
boulder slowly over grit
steel season claiming no one
mine a crust to hold
for summer.

Wide as walkable in a day
measure your head in my lap,
deep as a shallow dish or
perfect ball bearing roll, but not
in my meadow. Who needs
when sky gives away, no string.
Hit gently so I feel wind a little whip
so thankless midnight rain remembering.

THIS IS HOW HE LEFT ME

The body gives up his last, not to ever take another.
Lungs give out.
End the work in blowing, out puffing.
Born, beloved heart well-timbered.
Lately slows, steps weaken.
Days are blind, arms lame, no more rowing, never wield,
and now the beating storm lifts, rain my friend.
With himself he floats over the flood.
Rise like a bird not swept away.
To the end he climbs the cliff well-geared and goes.
His fingers gather whistling wind in this hollow,
guest and host bide in his little bed, where
       no other can be following.
The water rises leaves nothing behind but ash and longing for.

GOOD MORNING, DEATH

Good morning, Death.
First slanting light close over mine.
Shake, shake, and throw them down
words in my head, throw them down
like the sailors dice tell lies.

Good morning, Death. I will not die in Philadelphia
in May on a day it may, may not be raining.
I will not shake the lowest branch again,
blossoms spinning of a year.

Sudden shadow from the west and lightning
burrows in the roots, a sycamore down or dementia
sweeps away the hours and days well in advance of the worms.
I prefer not to know my last weather.

No more numbered seasons
I shake by the neck, shake, and shake
not just lapels but pelted body of a bear
in the jaws of a man tumbled down stairs
hammering, hammering on the ringing
tether against the pole, high and thin.

Fill a schoolyard, play or yesterday or the wind.

ANNIVERSARY

Why do the breast, the throat,
shoulders, cheekbones cry
rise from the gully of the gut
to sing in the fingers, buzz
my body as a bell of bone.

Waiting, warning tone rolls over,
trucks back up the tires
hesitate, stop at the crosswalk
going by.

That is what I breathe
unwanted oxygen
particles of you might
taste of mist, your thunder fluting
as awful rainbow
when you, my raft, went over
your Niagara that last honeymoon,
unmarrying me.

ELEGY

Dead husband, your handsome dark
wherever you stand just outside,
embrace me first, before then after
passing in and out of lamps at dusk.
Who's here? That's the question.
Ted Hughes - he scares me, him
and his dead wives and children.
I have a family. Don't look to
the black blood of their shadows.
If I look too soon I may want to follow.
Go down in the dark, bring you up home.

KINDS OF NOTHING

1.
Spread bedroll on a cot not mine.
Pillow and a head full of sound.

Four AM my lights on.
The poems don't care.
Storm coming.

2.
I lashed the grill
to the iron fence,
swept the wet leaves.

Hurricane season's up from Cuba,
just like you over me.

SEPTEMBER

The day doesn't last
as long as doors
don't close
light in the hall still on
crickets, the dark outside.

It can't be time to sleep, things
       still go on.
Even the thrum of
compressor at back of the fridge says
       something's
       going on.

Remember when we drove, into the
       night,
         tires on the road,
            rum.
You really
       should be here,
you
           really should be here.

A PLACE IN THE UNIVERSE

You who wanted
to tread barely touching, to swarm
rock leaving only chalk prints on stone
leap over tallis, alpine in your time disturb not a blade

exchanged the reddening smog of L.A.
for fog in the hands, in the fingers San Gabriel's chaparral.
Lightning to the asphalt to the tires on the road
burning skipped over. Through all of these

you breathed sweet weather patterns across me
nearly died three times
then you rose, giant, sky again around your knees
we wept and rambled all familiar places.

Traveling as if smoke
time makes a meal of your sinews, your sad songs and joy
of your will, makes muscles into leather then wax
even takes your excrement from you,
drowning man.

The pastor asked, atheist,
what do you. *A place*
in the universe.

I'll be lungs for us both
I gather you here.
If you're out there,
come in.

NOTES:

GOOD MORNING. The line "to lay me down one last time" is a lyric from the song To Lay Me Down by Jerry Garcia and Robert Hunter.

EARTH'S BODY. This ends with a quote from William Hill, an off-duty California state trooper, written by Jaymes Song and Mark Niesse of the Associated Press.

300 DAYS. The Japanese phrase *mono no aware* refers to the awareness of transience. It means "the pathos of things" and is pronounced AH-wah-reh.

GLACIAL ERRATICS SETTLED FOR A TIME. The line "me & you babe, how about it" paraphrases a lyric in Mark Knopfler's Romeo & Juliet

GOOD MORNING DEATH. This poem was inspired by César Vallejo's poem Black Stone on a White Stone.

ELEGY. The two quotes are from Ted Hughes's poem Moonwalk.

The Author

Jennifer Hook met her husband, Gary Ayres, in 1975 when they were freshmen at the University of California Santa Cruz. She studied painting with Neil Welliver at the University of Pennsylvania, earning an MFA in 1989. In 1991 she and Gary founded Hook & Ayres Design in Philadelphia. Their porcelain and silver jewelry has been sold at craft shows and museums throughout the northeast.

Since Gary's death in 2010, Jennifer has studied with Leonard Gontarek and is a member of his Osage Poets group. She has read her work at the Green Line Café Poetry Series Open Readings, as one of "Nine Philadelphia Poets for Change," and at Philly Poetry Day. This is her first book of poems.

www.ingramcontent.com/pod-product-compliance
Lightning Source LLC
Chambersburg PA
CBHW021002090426
42736CB00010B/1425